50 Things

Book Series

Reviews from Readers

I recently downloaded a couple of books from this series to read over the weekend thinking I would read just one or two. However, I so loved the books that I read all the six books I had downloaded in one go and ended up downloading a few more today. Written by different authors, the books offer practical advice on how you can perform or achieve certain goals in life, which in this case is how to have a better life.

The information is simple to digest and learn from, and is incredibly useful. There are also resources listed at the end of the book that you can use to get more information.
50 Things To Know To Have A Better Life: Self-Improvement Made Easy!
Author Dannii Cohen

This book is very helpful and provides simple tips on how to improve your everyday life. I found it to be useful in improving my overall attitude.
50 Things to Know For Your Mindfulness & Meditation Journey
Author Nina Edmondso

Quick read with 50 short and easy tips for what to think about before starting to homeschool.
50 Things to Know About Getting Started with Homeschool by Author Amanda Walton

---

I really enjoyed the voice of the narrator, she speaks in a soothing tone. The book is a really great reminder of things we might have known we could do during stressful times, but forgot over the years.
Author Harmony Hawaii

There is so much waste in our society today. Everyone should be forced to read this book. I know I am passing it on to my family.
50 Things to Know to Downsize Your Life: How To Downsize, Organize, And Get Back to Basics
Author Lisa Rusczyk Ed. D.

Great book to get you motivated and understand why you may be losing motivation. Great for that person who wants to start getting healthy, or just for you when you need motivation while having an established workout routine.
50 Things To Know To Stick With A Workout: Motivational Tips To Start The New You Today
Author Sarah Hughes

50 THINGS TO KNOW
ABOUT TRAVELLING AROUND
SPAIN
IN A CAMPERVAN

From Spanish Culture to
Becoming a Digital Nomad

Nicki Wylie

CZYK
PUBLISHING

CZYK Publishing Since 2011.
CZYKPublishing.com
50 Things to Know

Lock Haven, PA
All rights reserved.
ISBN: 9798767758944

50 THINGS TO KNOW ABOUT TRAVELLING AROUND
SPAIN IN A CAMPERVAN

BOOK DESCRIPTION

Are you thinking about travelling around Spain in your campervan, but worried about not speaking the language? Do you need practical advice from an experienced van lifer on how to budget for your campervan road trip around Spain? Would you like some insider tips on common issues you might face as a foreigner travelling by campervan in Spain and how to avoid them? If you answered yes to any of these questions, then this book is for you.

50 Things to Know About Travelling Around Spain in a Campervan by author Nicki Wylie offers an inside perspective into van life in Spain as a foreigner.

I've read a ton of books and travel guides about van life, but I missed that personal touch. I wanted to know more about the Author's own experience, their perspective, and the issues that they faced. First-hand experiences always resonate with me more, that's why I wanted to do something different with this book. Packed full of stories and tips from my own experiences of travelling around Spain in a campervan as an Irish expat, I wrote this book in the hopes that it becomes your North Star on your Spanish road trip adventure.

In these pages, you'll learn about the Spanish culture, get some boots-on-the-ground advice about van life in Spain, and pick up handy Spanish expressions to help you along the way. I'll also share my favourite van life spots, a few valuable lessons that I have learned from my own van dramas, and some insider tips to help you face common issues on the road.

TABLE OF CONTENTS

50 Things to Know

DEDICATION

For Helen & Brendan,

Who made this adventure possible and are with us every step of the way.

L.U.B.

ABOUT THE AUTHOR

Nicki Wylie is a Freelance Writer and full-time adventurer originally from Northern Ireland. Her passions are travelling, writing, learning new languages, and eating lots and lots of cheese. She speaks fluent Spanish and is dedicated to exploring every inch of the glorious Spanish countryside, one sangria at a time.

After spending six years living and working in Madrid as a Content Manager, she decided to pack it all in and go travelling around Spain full-time in a lovely little campervan with her partner (and Editor of this book) Richie, and their dog Bella. You can currently find her parked up somewhere in the Spanish countryside, writing, swimming in lakes with Bella, or having a cheeky siesta.

Since going full-time on the road, she's experienced amazing highs, a couple of lows, and some pretty hilarious van dramas. Who better to write a guide on van life in Spain? She wants to share everything she's learned with you to make your Spanish adventure one to remember (with as few van dramas as possible).

You can connect with Nicki on
LinkedIn @nicolajwylie or
visit her blog at afourwheelhome.com
to follow her adventures.

ABOUT THE EDITOR

Richie O'Connor is from Dublin, Ireland and has spent the last 11 years living and working in Spain. After working as an English teacher for several years, he moved into the world of editing books and online courses. His background in linguistics and a keen eye for detail made him a natural-born Editor. He speaks fluent Spanish and has been lucky enough to travel around the beautiful Spanish peninsula visiting as many places as possible.

He recently left the high-stress corporate world behind to follow his dreams of owning a campervan and living life on the road and he hasn't looked back since. His ideal day consists of making a delicious breakfast from the van, followed by a long walk anywhere in nature, chilling in his hammock after lunch with a cold beer and his guitar.

INTRODUCTION

"No road is long with good company."

— Turkish Proverb

ello and welcome to this guide on 50 things to Know About Travelling Around Spain in a Campervan. I wanted to start this book with a little bit about me, my partner (and Editor extraordinaire) Richie, and our van.

I wrote this book as a guide for people who own a campervan or are thinking about buying one and have Spain as their next road trip destination. If you don't currently have a campervan, don't let that stop you! Before moving to Spain, we spent two years travelling around Australia in a campervan. We started by renting one for six weeks to get a feel for it before buying our own. I highly recommend doing this so you can make sure van life is for you, get some handy hints on how to deck out your camper, and enjoy life on the road without worrying about breakdowns or pricey mechanics bills. It also means you can hit the road straight away.

After renting, we loved van life so much that we bought our own campervan in Australia. While it was fully kitted out and looked great, it broke down every time we went up a hill which —needless to say— was not ideal. After countless costly trips to the mechanic, we cut our losses and sold it for parts. On the bright side, we learned a valuable lesson; reliability is essential when buying a campervan.

Fast forward five years to May 2018 and we decided to buy another campervan, this time in Spain. We learned from our previous mistake and chose the most reliable van we could think of, the Ford Transit. After months of searching, we were lucky to find a 2016 Custom High Top model only thirty minutes from where we lived in Madrid. We didn't have a garden or parking space where we could work on the van (nor the space for the tools and materials needed to do it up). This, along with the time crunch to get it fitted out before summer, prompted our decision to pay a newly-established, local company to kit it out for us. In total, we paid €14,500 all in for the van and an extra €8,000 to *'camperize'* it. For that price, the company insulated the van, installed a 150W solar panel, a 115A auxiliary battery, a 300W DC to AC power inverter, a diesel heater, an extractor fan, all of our electrics, a sink with running water, a 50L grey water tank (this is where the water from our sink is deposited), x2 25L freshwater tanks, a 12V Dometic fridge, a portapotty, an awning, wooden flooring, and built-in overhead storage.

Since I work from the van, we opted for a table (with benches on either side) that folds down to a bed. However, in all honesty, we never use the bench format and would probably have been better going for a higher, fixed bed to give us a bit more storage space underneath. We use a portable gas stove with two rings which is great for both indoor and outdoor cooking. Since our kitchen area is small, we have a handy wooden cover over our sink to give us extra surface space. There is a small bench behind the passenger seat which stores our toilet, the power inverter, and cleaning products. It has a comfy foam top so that it doubles as extra seating and Bella's bed (although in the winter months, she usually manages to sneak into our bed and stretch herself out in the middle).

The van is a lot smaller than some of the campervans and motorhomes that you see on the road, but it's reliable, easy to manoeuvre, and it looks like a work van which is perfect for stealth camping. It's always nice having more space, but we have everything we need and we keep a small storage unit in Madrid for our extra possessions. I love having a high top van; being able to stand up straight maximises the space and allows us to easily cook inside the van when the weather's not great or there are mosquitoes around. It's worth noting that in several coastal towns around Spain, such as Cadaqués on the Costa Brava, larger vehicles such as motorhomes aren't allowed to enter the town.

You'll find more than just a few tips as you flick through these pages. I've added a few of my favourite van recipes to give you some cooking inspiration on your travels, a breakdown of what an average day in the van is like, and a playlist to get you in the travelling mood.

Thank you for buying this book, I'm so excited for you to start your van life journey in Spain and I hope this book inspires and helps you on your way. You never know, we might even see each other down the road.

Safe travels,
Nicki

ADVICE WHEN BUYING
YOUR FIRST CAMPERVAN

Buying your first campervan? My biggest piece of advice is to forget about aesthetics and think about how you will use your van. Put practicality first, and consider the following:

RELIABILITY

Will the vehicle be able to do the sort of travelling you want to do? Do you plan to do much off-road driving or cover large distances? I recommend factoring these questions into your decision-making process.

SIZE

How much space do you really need? Will you be carrying bikes or other sports equipment with you? If so, then you will need more storage space in your garage. Plan out which larger items you'll store there and get exact measurements so you can be sure they'll fit. It's tempting to go for the biggest option out there, however not only does that make it easier to accumulate too much stuff, but the extra weight will cost you more in fuel.

It's helpful to consider where you plan to stay in your van. If you plan to stay mostly in campsites, then a bigger campervan or motorhome will be more comfortable. On the other hand, if you want to do wild camping, a smaller van is a more practical purchase as you will be less conspicuous, providing more free camping options.

What's your budget and do you need extra money to renovate your campervan? Buying the best quality van you can afford is always wise, but I know people who have bought a van for less than €5,000 and have done it up themselves over time. If you go for a simple van with just the basics like a portable solar panel, battery-powered lights, and a sink that empties into a jerry can rather than a fixed water tank, you can convert a van into your home for around €500.

Don't get sucked into buying a load of gadgets and extras that you don't need; start minimal and buy as you go. At the end of this book, I have compiled a list of my essential items for van life which you can use as a starting point.

If you plan to design the layout of your campervan yourself, I recommend making a list of everything you will do in the van each day. Be specific and include everything from eating breakfast to switching off the lights before bed, that way you can make sure your van design reflects how you live.

SECTION 1: PREPPING FOR YOUR ROAD TRIP: CLIMATE, CULTURE, & CLOTHING

Spain is known for its hot summers and mild winters, making it an all-year-round van life destination. The majority of travellers have a limited window of when they can embark on their trip, making Easter week and the summer months (June - September) the most popular time of year to travel. In recent years especially, you'll find campervans (*'campers/furgonetas'*) and motorhomes (*'autocaravanas/ACs'*) from all over Europe dotted along the Spanish coastline during the summer months. Other travellers —usually full-time van lifers or retirees— prefer travelling in the shoulder seasons (April - May or October - December).

Spain is a big country and there's a huge difference in the weather in the north than in the Canary Islands, for example. If you plan to travel extensively in Spain, you'll need to pack for different weather conditions. On the other hand, if you plan to stay around one specific region, you might get away with packing less. Before you set off, check the weather along your route and pack accordingly. Many foreigners travelling to Spain make the mistake of thinking that Spain is always hot and sunny and end up not packing the right things.

Here are my top tips for preparing for your Spanish campervan trip.

Tip 1 - Travel In The Shoulder Seasons

My absolute favourite time to travel around Spain in my campervan is October and November. The weather is still lovely and mild in most parts of Spain (except the north which is already a little chilly), but without the stifling heat of summer. The evenings are still balmy enough to dine outside and the days are warm enough for a relaxing day on the beach. Since most people are back to work, campsites, motorhome areas, and national parks are usually quite empty.

Another reason why I love travelling in October is that the enforcement of the rules for where you can park your camper is more relaxed, meaning you can enjoy more wild camping. Of course, if you are a sun worshiper who isn't down with dipping in cooler water, then travelling during summer could be your ideal time. We recently spent 7 weeks travelling around the south of Spain in June and July, and found that July was very busy, campsites were pricier, and it was suffocatingly hot in several places around the east coast, such as Almería and Calpe. If you do decide to travel in the summer months, invest in a good handheld fan or travel towards the north.

Van Drama Alert

If travelling in October, don't underestimate how cold it can get in the van the further north you go. We spent a few incredibly chilly nights in Ávila and Salamanca in mid-October as we made our way to Portugal. Temperatures dropped to 1°C at night, prompting an emergency trip to sporting goods retailer Decathlon to buy some thermals. Luckily, we had our little heater on hand to stave off the chill.

Tip 2 - Pack smart

As I mentioned above, Spain's a big country and the climate varies greatly from region to region. If you're planning to travel extensively in Spain, visiting north and south, inland and coast, you'll need to pack for all weather conditions. We spent August around the Pyrenees in the north of Spain and it got chilly at night. I'd also recommend packing lots of light, breathable basics that you don't mind getting ruined, swimming gear and booties for rockier beaches, a sun hat, and a good pair of walking boots. Don't forget flip flops for showering in public showers!

If you're short on space, packing cubes are your friend. I have separate packing cubes for my tops, bottoms, and underwear which saves a heap of space and keeps me organised (ahem, sort of).

Van Drama Alert

Don't end up with a wardrobe of marshmallow pink clothes like me. Avoid whites and stick to clothes that can be washed together. You'll be doing your laundry in campsites or laundrettes on the road, so steer clear of hand wash-only clothes or delicates. The washing machines in laundrettes hold around 12 kilos of clothes, so you'll want to fit as much as possible in one machine. It costs around €3-5 to wash and €4-5 to dry.

TIP 3 - GET TO KNOW THE LOCAL VAN LIFE CULTURE IN SPAIN

Van life has really taken off in Spain. Unfortunately, in the past few years, the influx of van lifers has ruffled some feathers and new rules and restrictions have been put in place. Locals have complained about campervans and motorhomes leaving rubbish behind, going to the toilet outdoors leaving dirty toilet paper on the ground, emptying their wastewater in car parks, and ruining the landscape by blocking views of nature around coastal areas. Spain is still a van-friendly place, but I encourage all van lifers to do their part and always respect local rules. Here are just a few things to bear in mind:

- Leave no trace - Put your rubbish in the bin. If there are no bins, bring it with you and dispose of it when you can.
- Do NOT empty dirty dishwater from your sink (grey water) out in parks, car parks, or anywhere in nature. Look out for designated areas in campsites and service areas where you can empty your grey water and black water (toilet waste).
- If you really have to go to the bathroom outside, dig a hole and take your dirty toilet paper with

31

you, dumping it (excuse the pun) in the nearest bin.

- If you plan to shower outdoors using a solar shower, do it away from public places and ALWAYS use ecological shampoo and soap. Dumping water with chemicals such as shampoo, shower gel, or washing up liquid is damaging to local wildlife and is not legal.

Van Drama Alert

Keep your crumbs to yourself. We spent a few days sleeping for free in a small car park right on the beach just outside of Cabo de Gata national park in Almería (a must-see). In those few days, we saw two families wash their dishes in the beach shower, leaving egg and rice strewn all over the ground. This reflects badly on all van lifers and leads to crackdowns on wild camping near beaches. Beach showers are for rinsing off after a refreshing dip, not for last night's leftovers.

Tip 4 - Research Popular Van Life Spots In Spain

The van life movement is popular all across Spain, but there are a few areas in particular with a large concentration of campervans and motorhomes. During the high season, the north of Spain is very popular amongst van lifers looking to escape the heat of the south. Northern Spain is a huge area packed with beautiful beaches, picturesque landscapes, and scrumptious food. Add it to your bucket list immediately (you can thank me later). I highly recommend road tripping across the northern coast during the summer while the weather is good and (mainly) dry.

Andalucía is another popular spot for van lifers all year round. Its mild winters make it a great pick for van lifers, and even in high season, van lifers flock to the beaches around Cádiz and Huelva despite the mid-summer heat. The coast around Cádiz is a van lifer's paradise, with secluded beaches, stunning white-washed villages, and exquisite food at low prices.

Travelling around the Spanish islands, such as the Canary Islands and the Balearics, by campervan is a must. However, it's very tricky during the high season due to the massive influx of tourists. The best time to tour islands like Fuerteventura, Ibiza, and Formentera is around October/November or early June. It's less busy and parking restrictions are more relaxed, but there's still great weather and a buzzing van life community.

Tip 5 - Learn The Lingo

You don't need to speak Spanish to travel around Spain in your campervan, but picking up some helpful Spanish phrases will definitely enhance your trip. English is spoken almost everywhere in Spain, especially in campsites and coastal areas. From my personal experience, Spaniards are incredibly friendly and welcoming, so learning a bit of Spanish will help you to communicate with the locals and get the inside scoop on some lesser-known local gems.

In every section of this book, you'll find a list of a few handy Spanish vocabulary words and expressions to help you learn the lingo and travel like a local.

English	Spanish
Laundrette	*Lavandería*
Washing machine	*Lavadora*
Dryer	*Secadora*
High season / Low season	*Temporada alta/baja*
Easter week	*Semana Santa*

SECTION 2: DRIVING YOUR CAMPERVAN IN SPAIN

In this section, you'll find some useful hints and reminders for driving in Spain. Being behind the wheel in a foreign country is nerve-wracking, especially when your vehicle is also your home. Drivers in Spain can be a little reckless at times, often breaking the speed limits and making last-minute manoeuvres so it's important to keep your wits about you at all times. If you're prone to road rage, it's probably best to mentally prepare yourself in advance and leave yourself plenty of time to get to your next destination. I've found counting to ten helps.

Generally speaking, roads are excellent throughout Spain, and there aren't a huge amount of toll roads compared to other European countries like Portugal or France. Spain boasts a whopping 361,000 km of roads, including 15,000 km of motorways.

I've put together the most common information that you'll need to help you adjust to driving in Spain. Any information you find in this section (such as speed limits) is subject to change, so when in doubt, always do your own research and follow the instructions on road signs laid out by local authorities.

Here are my top tips for driving your campervan in Spain.

TIP 6 - GET TO KNOW THE BASIC RULES OF THE ROAD

If you're coming from the UK, Ireland, Australia, New Zealand, or South Africa it may take you a couple of days to get used to driving on the right. After almost seven years here, I still look the wrong way every time I cross the street. In Spain, you should always drive on the right, overtake on the left, and give priority to traffic coming from the right (except at roundabouts). Don't worry if your memory is anything like mine, the roads are generally well signposted to keep you right.

While most of the driving rules in Spain are similar to those in other European countries, you may find a few traffic rules that differ from your home country, especially on mountain roads. Keep in mind that priority changes on slopes with more than a 7% incline; vehicles going uphill have priority unless they are close to a place where they can pull in. It's also mandatory to beep your horn on blind bends when travelling on mountain roads in areas such as the Pyrenees or Picos de Europa (definitely worth a visit).

Van Drama Alert

You may come across a strange phenomenon known as phantom traffic jams on Spanish motorways. This doesn't only occur in Spain, but it's quite a common occurrence here as drivers tend to tailgate. It happens when a car slows down or brakes slightly causing the car behind to slow down even more. This has a knock-on effect, rippling through the line of traffic until it grinds to a halt for no apparent reason. Not great for the old road rage (see previous comment re: counting to ten).

Tip 7 - Learn The Different Types Of Roads

It's important to understand the signage for different roads when planning your trip (or playing 'Eye Spy'). In Spain, motorways are identified by an 'A' which stands for *'autovía'*, the Spanish word for "motorway". If you see a road marked 'AP' (*'autopista de peaje'*), this signals that you're about to enter a toll road. 'AP' is used to signal toll roads everywhere in Spain, except Madrid where toll roads are identified by an 'R' (which stands for *'radial'*).

When you come across toll barriers, or *'peajes'*, you will need to either take a ticket or pay a small toll. If you don't have the exact change, opt for the lane marked *'manual'*. If you're paying by card or you have the exact change, you can take the lane marked *'automático'*. You may also see a sign with a white T on a blue background which signals a teletoll (*'telepeaje'*). This lane is reserved for cars fitted with a special chip that tracks and takes toll payments automatically. The price of tolls varies depending on location, but you can expect to pay an average of between six cents and forty cents per kilometre. Most toll booths are manned and will accept cash or card.

Van Drama Alert

Don't get on the wrong side of the local neighbourhood watch! Look out for environmental zones in places like Madrid and Barcelona. These are zones where only residents are allowed to drive and they're usually indicated by a sign that reads *'Area de prioridad residencial'*. If you don't have a permit or special exemption, you could find yourself getting a hefty fine *('multa')* for driving in a prohibited zone.

TIP 8 - FAMILIARIZE YOURSELF WITH SPEED LIMITS & SIZE RESTRICTIONS

Always follow the speed limit marked on road signs, but if you're unsure, here are some general guidelines. The speed limit for vehicles weighing less than 3,500 kg is 90km/h on conventional roads and 120km/h on motorways. For vehicles weighing over 3,500 kg, it's 80 km/h on conventional roads and 90km/h on motorways.

Beware of height restrictions when driving in Spain, especially in car parks near the beach and supermarket car parks. You'll generally find more height restriction barriers *('gálibos')* than in other countries, preventing tall vehicles, such as motorhomes, from entering certain zones. Our van is 2.4m high and we rarely have issues, except when trying to fit under the covered areas in supermarket car parks which are generally 2.2m high.

When you think of Spain, you probably picture beautiful, whitewashed villages with narrow, cobbled streets. While narrow streets may be part of Spain's charm, it makes driving around towns and villages particularly tough for campervans and motorhomes. Keep this in mind when entering small towns and try to stick to main roads and car parks on the outskirts to avoid getting stuck. Narrow cobbled streets; the enemy of motorhomes and high heels alike.

Van Drama Alert

Most Spanish beaches have signs prohibiting large vehicles, especially motorhomes, from parking in that area so keep an eye out. Vehicles parked there risk getting clamped or towed. We saw a motorhome get clamped in a beach car park in Roses, Costa Brava where there was a sign prohibiting vehicles over 2.5m. Always toe the line on the coast (see what I did there?).

TIP 9 - PLAN AHEAD WHEN FUELLING UP

The cost of petrol in Spain is relatively low compared to other European countries. You will generally pay more for petrol at the bigger stations like Repsol, Cepsa, and BP and, of course, on toll roads. I recommend filling up in places like Carrefour (a large Spanish supermarket chain) and big shopping outlets where the price of petrol is normally more competitive. To give you an idea of how much you're likely to spend on fuel, I've calculated our total fuel costs for a month-long trip in Section 4 of this book.

Most petrol stations in Spain offer free air and water so we like to make the most of these to save us a trip to a motorhome area to fill up and empty. We don't drink this water, but we use it for doing the dishes, filling our solar shower, and washing our hands. A few petrol stations in Spain even have an area for campervans and motorhomes to dispose of black and grey water free of charge, so look out for those when you stop off to fuel up.

Van Drama Alert

Make sure you have enough gas to last you during your trip. It's illegal to fill up foreign gas canisters *('bombonas de gas')* in Spain and you need ID and proof of address to buy a Spanish one. If you run out of gas and are unable to fill up your canister, you have two options: Look for a second-hand Spanish gas canister in second-hand shops *('rastros')* or find a shop that sells Campingaz gas canisters. Anyone can buy these without proof of address.

TIP 10 - LEARN THE LINGO

Here are some driving-related words and phrases to help you on your way.

English	Spanish
Road	*Carretera*
Fill (up) fuel tank	*Repostar*
Diesel/Unleaded	*Diesel, gasóleo/Sin plomo*
Have a nice trip!	*¡Buen viaje!*
Driving licence	*Carnet (de conducir)*

SECTION 3: WHERE TO STAY ON THE ROAD

In this section, I'll share some ideas on how to find your next awesome sleeping spot. I'll go through the different camping options available to you while on the road in Spain and give you an idea of what facilities you can expect to find at each one.

In Spain, there is a distinction between sleeping in your vehicle *('pernoctar')* and camping *('acampar')*. You're generally allowed to park and sleep in your vehicle anywhere there's a suitable parking space and no signs prohibiting large vehicles or overnight parking. You can eat, sleep, and cook inside your vehicle, but you can't convert the parking space into a 'motorhome pitch'. Essentially, it means that you need to be parked within one parking space without any objects hanging from or left outside your vehicle, as this would be considered camping. This is enforced more in some areas than others and is one of the times when having a campervan that looks like a work van pays off dividends (I often remind myself of this when I have van envy).

As we're pretty self-sufficient in our campervan, we try to camp for free the majority of the time. We normally stop off for a night in a campsite or motorhome area around once a week for a hot shower (hot showers are the only luxury I miss from my old life) and to do some van maintenance. The rest of the time, we use our solar shower for a quick rinse if we're in a quiet place. If your campervan doesn't have a shower or hot water and you don't fancy paying for somewhere to stay, another option is to buy a month-to-month *('sin permanencia')* gym membership that covers the whole of Spain. I didn't go for this option because we tend to avoid big towns and cities where most of the gym franchises can be found (I've also dedicated most of my life to avoiding the gym).

Tip 11 - Know The Rules Of Roadside Or Wild Camping

While it may be allowed under some conditions, generally speaking, wild camping is prohibited in Spain and totally prohibited in national parks or within 6 metres of any natural water source (like a river, a lake, or the sea). Spain is divided into 17 autonomous communities, each one with their own rules and regulations around wild camping. Some provinces police this very strictly, while others are more lax. Checks are stricter and more frequent during the high season, especially near coastal areas and in national parks. Don't let this put you off though, it just means that sometimes you may have to spend the day at a beautiful spot and then drive to a nearby car park or designated motorhome area to sleep. Alternatively, you could look for more secluded spots to park up, which is all part of the fun. I love wild camping when I can; you get to go fully off the grid, wake up in the heart of nature, and it's completely free. I especially love it when I'm not working and can enjoy having no phone signal or internet. It's the perfect way to disconnect.

We use the Park4Night app to find free camping spots on the road. The places posted on the app are tried and tested by other van lifers and you can find ratings and reviews of each location. It's been an absolute lifesaver for us on the road and we've found some unforgettable places thanks to it. It's also super useful if you're on a shorter trip and don't have the time to hunt out your own spots. If you're going really off the grid, especially off-season, I recommend going searching for your own wild camping locations. It's all part of the adventure.

Cost:

Free

Services:

None (some places may have a bin, water tap, or toilets)

Van Drama Alert

We've only been moved on twice during our time on the road. Of course, both times happened on the same night. We parked up in the car park of La Isleta Del Moro beach in Cabo de Gata only to get moved on by park rangers at 11 pm. We drove a few kilometres away to Los Escullos beach (where we'd previously stayed for several days with no issues) but got moved on by the same ranger an hour later. We ended up sleeping in a Lidl car park. Not quite as idyllic, but great for grabbing some fresh rolls in the morning. Sometimes it's just the luck of the draw.

TIP 12 - SEARCH FOR DESIGNATED FREE CAMPING AREAS

If you want the scenic views of wild camping but you're not sure where to do it, I'd recommend searching for designated free camping areas (*'área/zona de acampada libre'*) on your route. The quality of the camping zone varies from place to place, but you will find plenty dotted around Spain where you can relax and camp without worrying about being moved on. Many of these designated camping areas are located close to hiking trails, mountains, or rivers making them a great spot for unwinding in nature for a day or two. We found a great camping area in Yátova, Valencia (39.4010371, -0.7988926) that had toilets, outdoor BBQs, and a tap, but it comes down to luck so come prepared for minimal services.

Cost:
Free
Services:
Apart from bins, there are usually little to no services available, but it depends on the place.

Van Drama Alert

If you're using Park4Night, try to check on Google Earth to see what the access roads are like. We ended up getting stuck in the sand on our way to an overnight spot in Cullera, south of Valencia. It was dark and we followed our GPS right onto the beach (whoops!). Luckily, we managed to free ourselves using some planks of wood and didn't have to get towed, but it was a close call.

TIP 13 - MOTORHOME AREAS ARE A MORE AFFORDABLE ALTERNATIVE TO CAMPSITES

We usually look out for motorhome areas *('Áreas de Servicio para Autocaravanas')* when we want to stop off for a hot shower and electricity. Motorhome areas are somewhere in between designated free camping areas and campsites. They're generally cheaper than campsites, but still have all the facilities we need; showers, an area to empty and fill up, and electricity *('luz')* if I am working a lot or the solar panel hasn't seen much sun. You usually pay extra for a plot with electricity. We've even come across a few self-service motorhome areas where you check-in and out via a machine and you can use the machines to pay for services like hot water.

The cost and quality of motorhome areas differ greatly from place to place, but you can always check the Park4Night app or Google Maps for reviews and to see what facilities are on offer. We stayed in one near Torrevieja, Murcia which cost around €15 per night in the high season and €9 in the low season. After a trip to the San Pedro del Pinatar mud baths, we were in desperate need of a shower (the mud may have restorative properties, but it smells like rotten eggs). This motorhome had super clean toilets, hot showers, electricity, Wi-Fi, a laundry room, water taps *('grifos de agua')*, a bar and restaurant, and areas to empty and fill water. Other motorhome areas are more basic and may provide cold showers, toilets, and a tap.

Cost: €0 - 20 per night (the cost depends on the time of year, location, and facilities available).

Services:

The services available in motorhome areas vary depending on the region and the price.

Van Drama Alert

Make sure you have enough cash *('efectivo')* including change (*'cambio'*) before checking into a self-service motorhome area. We spent a few days in a lovely one on the outskirts of Barcelona and realised when we tried to check out that cards weren't accepted and we didn't have enough cash to cover it. The gates were closed and the nearest ATM (*'cajero'*) was a twenty-minute walk away. Luckily, a fellow van lifer lent us money so we could pay, drive into town to take out cash, and loop back to return the money. Thanks, friend!

TIP 14 - LOOK FOR DEALS ON LONG-TERM STAYS AT CAMPSITES

Spain has a great selection of campsites, especially around the coastal regions. Campsites, or *'campings'* in Spanish, are more expensive than the other options in this section, but they tend to have more facilities and are located closer to cities, beaches, or other popular landmarks. Campsites are generally clean and well-kept with 24/7 security. Some of the larger ones are like their own resorts with restaurants, shops, sports facilities, swimming pools, sports equipment rental, and entertainment during the high season.

Campsites are much cheaper outside of the high season and offer special rates for long-term stays. If you plan to explore one particular region of Spain for a longer period, you can get a great deal on a campervan pitch *('parcela')* and use it as your base.

Cost:
€20 - €50 per night during the high season
€12 - €30 per night during the low season

Services:

Most campsites offer a full range of services included in the price.

TIP 15 - LEARN THE LINGO

These words and phrases should come in handy when you're looking for your next sleeping spot in Spain.

English	Spanish
Where can I empty my grey water/black water?	*¿Dónde puedo vaciar las aguas grises/las aguas negras?*
How much is it for one night?	*¿Cuánto es la noche?*
Where are the bins?	*¿Dónde están los contenedores? / ¿Dónde está la basura?*
Are you allowed to sleep here overnight?	*¿Se puede pernoctar / pasar la noche aquí?*
Is there a campsite/motorhome area near here?	*¿Hay un camping/una área de autocaravanas por aquí?*

SECTION 4: BUDGETING FOR YOUR TRIP

Planning your Spanish road trip is fun. Budgeting for it is less fun, but a very important step. One of my biggest concerns about living in the campervan full-time was budgeting; how much I would need to earn and how much my expenses would be. I really wanted to dedicate a section in this book to how much we spend in an average month to give you a realistic idea of what to expect. Of course, everyone is different and how much you spend will depend on many factors including the type of trip you're taking, whether you plan to eat out a lot if you're going to wild camp or stay in paid accommodation, and how many miles you're going to clock up. Even still, it's good to have a benchmark in mind.

To give you the most accurate estimate possible, I've calculated our total expenses during a month-long trip and broken them down into categories. We took this trip in August 2021, starting from Madrid heading north towards Burgos, moving east towards La Rioja, then across the Spanish side of the Pyrenees, and down through the Costa Brava, passing through Barcelona and back to Madrid (just over 2,100kms).

We treated this trip as more of a holiday, staying in motorhome areas more often than normal and eating out regularly (it would be rude not to, right?), so we spent a little more than usual. Travelling in the summer, the rates for motorhome areas were higher too. When it comes to budgeting for your trip, my advice is to always err on the side of caution and set aside extra funds in case of van dramas like break-ins, breakdowns, or breakups. Creating a daily or weekly budget is essential for long-term travellers, but if you are only spending a few weeks on the road I say relax a little and just enjoy the experience.

This was our route. We wanted to make more stops but, as always, time got away from us.

In this section, you'll see a breakdown of our costs for this 31-day trip. This includes accommodation, groceries, petrol, and eating out costs. The amounts I've listed are the total spending for the three of us (Bella included). I have removed a few miscellaneous costs such as phone plans and subscriptions to Spotify and Netflix (€102 per month), and our storage unit (€30 per month).

Tip 16 - Have A Contingency Plan For Accommodation Costs

When working out your budget, don't forget that your van is your home. If it needs repair work or is stolen, you need enough money to pay for alternative accommodation on top of repair costs, so set extra money aside just in case. Accommodation costs are a relatively low expense for us on the road. This route included a few bigger towns and cities on the Costa Brava and we didn't want to leave the van unattended, so we stayed in paid motorhome areas more often than we typically do. We stayed in paid motorhome areas 7 times during the trip, totalling just under €90.

As they're slightly pricier, we typically don't stay in many campsites unless they're in a great location. However, if we do splash out on a campsite with ample facilities like a swimming pool or gym, we aim to arrive as early as we can so we have plenty of time to make the most of them (it's the only time in my life I arrive anywhere early). Travelling so much can get tiring after a while and it's important to know when to rest. When we feel ourselves getting tired, we splash out on a nice motorhome area or campsite and stay for a few days (or as long as we need) to relax and recharge.

Moving to a new spot every day is exciting on a short-term trip, but every so often I need a few days in one place to reset. I think it's an important lesson for full-time van lifers to learn.

Number of nights in paid accommodation: 7
Total spending: €87
Average cost per place: €12.50

Van Drama Alert

Always have a financial buffer in case of van dramas. Our storage unit flooded a few days after we got it. We came back to grab a few last-minute items the day we were hitting the road and everything was soaking. Luckily, we packed everything in vacuum pack bags so only a few books were ruined and the mould hadn't set in yet. If you're using a storage unit and don't want furry clothes, put a pallet on the floor to keep boxes off the ground and waterproof everything. If you can, give a friend a spare key just in case.

Tip 17 - Be Realistic About Your Grocery Budget

One of our biggest expenses on the road is food. I adore food and I love having the van well-stocked. Our fridge is quite small, so we can only really keep about four days' worth of groceries in there at best. We usually pop in to get groceries every four or five days and eat out several times a week (more on that later). Spanish supermarkets are pricier than local shops such as fruit and veg shops (*'fruterías'*), bakeries (*'panaderías'*), and butcher's (*'carnicerías'*) so we shop local when we can. Having said that, even though the larger supermarket chains like Carrefour, Mercadona, Aldi, and Lidl are more expensive, they're more accessible than smaller, local shops and have better parking.

If the following seems quite expensive to you, that's because it is. Groceries are relatively cheap in Spain and you could most definitely feed two people for a week for €40 to €50 (around €200 per month). I see food as my biggest luxury item and I don't mind forking out extra money to eat well. This total includes Bella's food and dog treats.

Number of grocery shops: 10
Total spending: €280
Average cost per shop: €28

TIP 18 - CALCULATE HOW MUCH PETROL YOUR CAMPERVAN USES & BUDGET ACCORDINGLY

How much you spend on fuel will depend on how many miles you plan to cover. We always keep an eye out for cheaper fuel rates and fill our tank (around €90) when we come across one. A full tank gets us roughly 900km, so it's pretty economical. If your campervan guzzles fuel or you intend to cover more ground, you may need to budget higher for fuel costs.

On our month-long trip, we covered just over 2,000 km for a total of €247, including toll fees. This was quite a lot of driving over different terrain; motorways, mountain roads, and back roads near the coast.

Number of fill-ups: 3
Total spending: €247
Average cost per fill-up: €82

TIP 19 - LOOK FOR WAYS TO EAT OUT FOR LESS

Dining out was by far our biggest expense on this leg of our trip. I prefer eating out for lunch and cooking breakfast and dinner in the van. Almost every restaurant in Spain offers a reasonably priced lunch menu (*'menú del día'*) that comes with 2 courses, dessert and a glass of wine *('una copa de vino')* or a small glass of beer *('una caña')*. It goes without saying, steer clear of super touristy spots when you're searching for a restaurant as you tend to pay more for less.

In Spain, you usually get something to nibble on when you order a drink. Proper *tapas* (the free ones) are no longer common outside of Andalucía, but you'll normally be served a small plate of olives, nuts, or crisps with each drink. Keep an eye out for local tapas fairs and food festivals on your travels to sample top-class Spanish cuisine for reasonable prices.

If you're on a shoestring budget, look for meal deals or websites where you can buy food that is going to be thrown out at a discounted price. In the major cities like Barcelona or Madrid, you can order a bag of food that hasn't been sold by restaurants and pick it up at the end of lunch service or dinner service. Not only is it great value and low waste, but it's mostly from good-quality restaurants and markets that simply don't want to waste good food. You can get a tasty, cooked meal for around €5.

Number of times we ate out: 20
Total spending: €410
Average cost per meal (for two people, including drinks): €20.50

Grand Total:

Accommodation	€87
Grocery shopping	€280
Transport	€247
Bars and Restaurants	€410
Total Cost (2 people, 1 dog, 1 month):	**€1, 024**

TIP 20 - LEARN THE LINGO

Here are a few money-related words and phrases to help you stay on budget during your road trip.

English	Spanish
How much does it cost?	*¿Cuánto vale? / ¿Cuánto cuesta? / ¿Cuánto es?*
I'd like the lunch menu, please.	*Yo quiero el menú del día, por favor.*
Can I pay by card?	*¿Puedo pagar con tarjeta?*
Can I have the bill, please?	*¿Me traes la cuenta, por favor?*
A table for two, please.	*Una mesa para dos, por favor.*

SECTION 5: TRAVELLING WITH YOUR FURRY FRIEND

Travelling with your pet is amazing. I can't imagine living in the van without Bella (she's a great security alarm too). As much as travelling with your furry friend is worth it, there are a few factors to bear in mind before you set off. Make sure you have all the relevant documentation for your pet, take them to the vet for a checkup before you hit the road, and pack a long leash and a muzzle if you're travelling with a dog. Having your pet on board also takes up a bit more living space in your campervan. I recommend having a dedicated area for them in the van that they know is their space.

Bella is a healthy, happy dog, but she has had a few van dramas of her own during our travels. We were slightly nervous at the beginning because she's quite a sensitive dog who struggles to relax, but she absolutely loves van life. A day in the life of Bella usually consists of running around in the mountains or at the beach, taking naps in the sun, exploring new towns and cities, and snuggling up on her little bed in the evenings. As an adopted dog, she has always been quite hesitant around other dogs but she is slowly but surely getting more confident and has even made a few doggy friends along the way (she still doesn't share her toys though).

If you want your pet to tag along on your Spanish road trip, you'll find a wealth of useful advice in this section to ensure that your furry best friend is happy, healthy, and safe during your travels.

Tip 21 - Sort Out Pet Documentation For Your Trip A Month In Advance

If your pet *('mascota')* is coming along on your Spanish campervan adventure, you must have all the necessary documentation with you. For peace of mind, invest in pet insurance that covers the whole of Spain (or Europe if you plan to travel outside of Spain). I'd recommend making an appointment with your vet a month before you plan to start your trip to confirm what documentation you'll need and to make sure your pet has a total bill of health before setting off.

I've created a small checklist of what we did to get Bella ready for life on the road:

- Get your pet an up-to-date EU Pet Passport (we bought Bella's at our local vet for €18).
- Make sure that your pet is microchipped and that the correct information is on their chip.
- Check that all of your pet's vaccines are up to date (you'll need to do this at least 21 days before you travel).
- If your pet takes any medication, ask your vet to prescribe enough to last you for the trip.
- Confirm with your vet if you need to take any other relevant documentation for your pet.

When we took Bella to the vet before we began our trip, the vet gave us three extra months of deworming tablets and prescribed anti-inflammatory medication, just in case. We keep the van stocked with some ear drops and the extra prescriptions on the off-chance that Bella gets sick while we're far away from a vet or at the weekend when most vets are closed. Ask your vet for advice on the types of medication your dog *('perro')* might need or what precautions you should take while in Spain.

Tip 22 - Get Your Pet A Collar To Protect Against Parasites

Once you have all the necessary documentation and your pet's vaccines are up to date, you should have no problem visiting the vet on your trip (although fingers crossed that won't be necessary). If your pet is feeling under the weather and you need to take it to the vet (*'el veterinario'),* look online for vets in the area, check reviews to make sure they come recommended and call to try to make an appointment *('pedir hora/cita')*. In many parts of Spain, your vet may speak English which will make the process a lot easier.

If your dog is in good health, the most common issues you may run into on the road are insects. Ticks and lice are common in certain parts of Spain and can be extremely dangerous for your pet. They're usually most prevalent in warmer, humid areas such as in the south of Spain. The good news is that there is a special collar that can help to protect your pet from parasites and parasitic diseases like leishmaniasis (found in southern Europe). Bella wears one of these collars by a brand called "Seresto" which costs €35 from our local vet and lasts for six months.

Van Drama Alert

After a few days of wild camping in the mountains and playing with some other local dogs, we discovered Bella had caught fleas. As you can imagine, treating a dog with fleas in a van is no easy feat. We had to take her to the vet who gave her a one-dose pill, spray everything down with flea spray, wash all of our clothes and bedding, and then wash Bella. Since that not so pleasant experience, we keep the flea spray on hand to spray Bella down when we've been to places where pesky mites, fleas, or ticks might be lurking.

TIP 23 - LEARN THE GENERAL DOG ETIQUETTE IN SPAIN

Spain is a very dog-friendly country and most dog owners will bring their pet pooch with them when they eat out or go for a few drinks. It's important to know the general dog etiquette when travelling with your pet, so I've put together a list of a few common guidelines to help you:

- Dogs are allowed on most outdoor terraces, but usually not indoors.
- Each of Spain's autonomous communities has slightly different rules, but generally speaking, dogs should always be on a lead in public areas.
- Dogs can travel on the metro and intercity trains as long as they're on a lead *('correa')* and wearing a muzzle *('bozal')*.
- While it's not a legal requirement, it's a general obligation in Spain to strap your dog in using a dog belt or harness while you're driving. If your dog stays in the back of your campervan, I recommend securing it safely with a harness in case you have to brake suddenly.

One of the most important things to do before your trip is to check if your dog is considered a dangerous dog in Spain. The Spanish government has a list of potentially dangerous dogs, known as '*perros potencialmente peligrosas*' (PPP) in Spanish. Pitbull terriers, rottweilers, Staffordshire bull terriers, and American Staffordshire terriers are among the dog breeds on the PPP list. The list varies from region to region, so you'll need to check online before you travel to different Spanish regions. If your dog is considered a dangerous dog, by law it has to wear a muzzle and be on the lead at all times. It must also be microchipped, insured, fully vaccinated, and have a valid dog licence.

Van Drama Alert

To avoid run-ins with the police, my advice is to carry a spare water bottle when you're in big cities with your pet, especially in hot weather. While in Cádiz, we were stopped by the police for not spraying the street after Bella did a pee. It's obligatory to spray water after your dog urinates in public places to avoid stains or smells. The police officer who stopped us was very nice once he realised that we didn't know the rules and it was an accident (excuse the pun).

TIP 24 - DOGS ARE ONLY ALLOWED ON DOG BEACHES DURING THE SUMMER

Taking your furry friend to the beach during the high season can be tricky. Most town/city councils have strict rules about having dogs on beaches during the busy period between June and the end of September. The good news is that there are plenty of dog beaches *('playas caninas')* in Spain, especially around the south, that are just for dogs and their humans. If you can't find a dog beach in the area, try to find a wild beach with no lifeguard. Wilder, less accessible beaches aren't usually patrolled by local rangers so you have less chance of running into issues. Outside of the high season, most beaches allow dogs, but certain beaches only allow dogs on leads or dogs that are registered in the area, so keep your eyes peeled for prohibition signs or you could face a hefty fine.

We managed to find loads of lovely dog beaches on our travels where Bella was able to swim and play fetch on the beach to her heart's content (she hasn't quite mastered the fetch part yet, but she loves running after her ball). If you can't find a dog beach, why not explore further inland? Spain has lots of rivers and lakes which are perfect for both you and your pooch to take a dip without any issues. Beach days are fun, just remember that the Spanish sun is strong, even in winter. Take plenty of water for your dog and find a cool, shady spot to shelter from the hot sun.

TIP 25 - LEARN THE LINGO

If you plan to travel with your pet pooch, the following words and phrases will be useful:

English	Spanish
Where is the nearest vet?	*¿Dónde está el veterinario más cercano?*
Can I have a bowl of water for my dog, please?	*¿Me traes un cubo / un poco de agua para mi perro, por favor?*
My pet is sick	*Mi mascota está enferma.*
My dog is lost	*Mi perro está perdido./Mi perro se ha perdido.*
Are dogs allowed?	*¿Se permiten los perros?*

SECTION 6: WORKING ON THE ROAD

Spain is a super popular destination for digital nomads. Sunshine, great food, and a laid back lifestyle, who wouldn't want to be a digital nomad in Spain? After spending a couple of years working with a hybrid approach —two days remote and three days in the office— I quit my 9 to 5 and decided to work for myself. It was a nerve-wracking decision, but the best one I've ever made. I have always enjoyed working in an office environment and was worried I'd feel isolated working from the van, but I love it. Being able to set my own schedule, choose the projects I take on, and have a new office every day is worth it for me.

So how did I do it? After working as a Content Manager for several years, I realised that I would struggle to do certain parts of my job from the van. I needed a lot of bandwidth for video editing, I used loads of different software, and my days were usually packed with meetings. While I loved my job, I would have been very restricted in where we could go and my schedule would have remained very much the same 9 to 5. So, I decided to take one of the parts of my job that I enjoyed the most —writing— and make that my career. Writing from the van is perfect as I don't need many tools or software and I can get by with pretty basic

79

internet coverage. I rarely have meetings now except when I start a new project and I can set my own hours as long as I hit my deadlines. After a few months of working as a Freelance Copywriter, I was able to earn enough to cover my expenses in the van. While my salary is considerably lower than it was before, so are my expenses. It may not be for everyone, but for me, I love the freedom I have being my own boss and deciding for myself when to take on more work and when to say no (something that has never come easy to me). In the next chapter of our van life journey, my goal is to dedicate more time to writing books and other types of content that truly inspire me.

If you are contemplating going full-time in your campervan but you're worried about the financial aspect, I get it. I was too. My advice is to be realistic. I started finding writing work for myself a few months before we began our van life adventure so I knew I had a small but steady source of income. Have a safety net to fall back on in case it takes you longer than expected to find an income, and most importantly, have faith in yourself. Once you remove the financial burden of monthly rent or mortgage payments, bills, and city expenses you'll find that you need a lot less to live on than you think. Life is short, take the plunge. Just get your ducks in order first. I hope this section gives you some insight into the life of a digital nomad working from a campervan in Spain.

TIP 26 - GET INSPIRATION: FIGURE OUT WHAT JOBS YOU CAN DO FROM YOUR VAN

I've met lots of fellow digital nomads on my travels who are living and working from their campervan. The more people I meet, the more different income options I hear about. For me, I wanted to choose a job that I'm passionate about and that gives me space to be creative. For others, flexibility is their top priority.

Here are a few ideas of jobs you can easily do from your campervan, based on my own experiences from my travels and those of the people I've met along the way.

CONSULTANCY WORK

I've met several full-time van lifers in Spain who are funding their travels with consultancy work. One van lifer used her social media channels to become a Vanlife Consultant and now offers consultancy sessions to people who want to take the plunge and go full-time in their van. It's not a path you can forge overnight, but if you have expertise in a specific area and an entrepreneurial mind, you can turn your knowledge and passion into your career. Since this type of work requires more video calls and meetings, you may have to pick destinations with decent internet coverage, but they are abundant in Spain.

WRITER

Writing is possibly the original remote job. If you love putting pen to paper and know your way around SEO, there are plenty of opportunities for freelance writers out there. I contribute to corporate blogs, write SEO articles, compose guest blog posts, and write copy for websites. Although the opportunities for earning are smaller than in other remote jobs, the flexibility and freedom it offers are priceless and I love it.

CONTENT CREATOR

We're now in the content creator golden era. If you're a dab hand at social media and you want to document your van life adventures, there are a myriad of opportunities to make money as a Content Creator. It's not an overnight job either though, you'll need to build a following and create reams of compelling content. A word of warning, YouTube is inundated with van life channels so you'll need to find a niche to give yourself an edge and stand out in a saturated market. Making a living as a Content Creator or Influencer is harder than it looks, but if you're prepared to put the hours in, the rewards can be huge.

ONLINE TUTOR

I've met quite a few van lifers who teach online or work as an Online Tutor. They teach languages, tutor kids, or give online classes on everything from coding to macramé. As long as you have reliable internet, you can earn pretty good money as an online teacher and set your own schedule. There are a whole host of teaching or skill-sharing platforms that you can sign up for to find students and promote yourself as a teacher.

SEASONAL WORKER

If sitting in front of a laptop isn't your thing—or you chose to pursue van life to get away from that lifestyle—then there are some other options out there to make money. Look out for seasonal jobs like farm work, fruit picking, hostel work, or even working at a ski resort. We took on seasonal jobs in Australia to fund our travels and, even though we didn't earn much money, we got to work outside, save enough to fund our trip, and I even learned how to snowboard (well, sort of). Spain has seasonal work all year round, it's just a case of speaking to locals or looking online to find one that suits your skills and expectations. I've met several van lifers who work on fruit farms during harvesting season and travel for the rest of the year, picking up odd jobs when needed.

TIP 27 - PICK A DATA PLAN THAT WORKS FOR YOUR JOB

There are two essential items you'll need to work on the road; a laptop *('portátil')* and an unlimited data plan. I pay €35.99 a month for unlimited calls and data and I have no complaints so far. If your telephone provider is outside of Spain, make sure that you choose a plan that offers unlimited data when roaming and double-check your tariff is included. Another option is to buy a prepaid *('prepago')* SIM card when you get to Spain from one of the big phone companies and top it up as you go. For €20/month, you can get in the region of 35 to 50 GB of data.

I use hotspot tethering for working, which works perfectly but does drain your battery. Spain is a perfect destination for digital nomads with the vast majority of towns and cities having fast 4G or 5G internet.

Coworking spaces have been popping up all over Spain in recent years, so you can always find a place with reliable internet to work in peace.

Van Drama Alert

As I mentioned, check your data plan with your network provider before you travel to make sure that you don't have to pay extra roaming costs. I recently learned the hard way that even though I have unlimited data in Spain, in Portugal I only have an allowance of 20GB per month. I ended up paying a fortune for going over my data limit.

TIP 28 - HUNT OUT THE FREE WI-FI SPOTS

If you fancy a change of scenery and don't want to work from your campervan, most public places like restaurants, coffee shops, and supermarkets have free Wi-Fi hotspots. Every so often, I like to take my laptop to a coffee shop or bar to grab a drink and charge up while I work. Just don't forget your headphones *('auriculares')*, Spanish bars and coffee shops tend to be loud.

Motorhome areas and campsites usually offer free Wi-Fi, but in my experience, the connection is quite slow and unreliable. If, like me, you hate nothing more than slow Wi-Fi, I'll let you in on a little trick. Find where the routers are located (they're usually near toilet blocks or kitchen areas) and try to park close by so you get a better Wi-Fi signal. Most bigger campsites have communal indoor areas with tables and chairs and Wi-Fi which make for great offices.

TIP 29 - RESEARCH THE BEST DIGITAL NOMAD SPOTS IN SPAIN

I couldn't write a section about working from your campervan without sharing some of my favourite places to be a digital nomad. If I have a busy working week coming up, I'll usually try to park up near a great digital nomad destination. For me, my criteria include a fast internet connection, a wide variety of coffee shops and coworking spaces, a good digital nomad community that has networking events, lots to see and do in my downtime, and a town or city with safe places to park the van. I'm a beach person, so my perfect nomadic office also has an ocean view and the smell of salt in the air.

It wasn't easy, but I've managed to pick my top two places to work remotely in Spain (trust me, it was a long list). Don't just take my advice though, the best way to scope out awesome remote working spots is by joining digital nomad groups on social media and connecting with other like-minded individuals.

TARIFA, CÁDIZ

Tarifa, in the southernmost part of Spain, is located where the Atlantic and Mediterranean meet. It has its own climate and is a hugely popular kitesurfing destination. It also has plenty of safe parking options for the van which is always a top priority. Tarifa is a perfect spot for digital nomads thanks to its fast internet, excellent array of top-class coworking spaces, and buzzing nightlife. When you're not working, you can explore the charming old town, stroll along the seafront, or take a kitesurfing lesson. A word of warning, it gets seriously windy there. In recent years, the digital nomad community has taken off in Tarifa and there are weekly events for remote workers who want to meet new people. I'd recommend joining the Tarifa Community Noticeboard group on social media before your stay to find out about upcoming events and notices.

JAVEA

I'm not much of a city person, but I do like to meet people on the road. That's why I think Javea is a perfect spot for digital nomads, campervan or no campervan. Javea is a beautiful town south of Valencia and well connected to other great destinations on the Costa Blanca. There are lots of things to do in Javea and neighbouring Dénia to keep you occupied when you aren't working and you'll even find a few places to park your campervan for free. One of the main reasons why Javea has become a popular destination for digital nomads across Europe is the increasingly popular co-living space Sun and Co. With beautiful coastal views, sunny weather, and a remote-work friendly vibe, Javea is a great place to park up for a few days or weeks.

TIP 30 - LEARN THE LINGO

Here are some top Spanish phrases to help you become a digital nomad in Spain. Good luck! *('¡Buena suerte!')*.

English	Spanish
What's the Wi-Fi password?	*¿Cuál es la contraseña de la WIFI? (pronounced /wee - fee/)*
Can I charge my laptop here?	*¿Puedo cargar mi portátil aquí?*
Is there a co-working space near here?	*¿Hay un espacio de coworking por aquí?*
Can I work from here?	*¿Puedo trabajar desde aquí?*
The Wi-Fi isn't working.	*No funciona la WIFI.*

SECTION 7: ISSUES ON THE ROAD

Van dramas are part and parcel of the van life experience, so try and embrace them. Just think, it's a funny story you can tell people for years to come. On a more serious note, running into issues on the road when you're abroad can be stressful and harder to deal with. My main goal with this section is to put your mind at ease and give you a few handy tips to help you navigate any potential van dramas or maybe even avoid them.

We've experienced almost every van drama possible —breakdowns, near accidents, illnesses, noisy van neighbours— and it hasn't tainted our view of van living in the slightest. The reality is that these things could happen anywhere and they're generally few and far between. My biggest advice is to go with your gut. If you park up somewhere and get a bad vibe, keep driving. If we get to an area late or I'm worried it's not the safest place to spend the night, then we'll move on and look for a spot where other motorhomes and campervans are parked (safety in numbers and all that). In the next few pages, I'll break down what to do if you run into common issues on the road such as breakdowns, break-ins, accidents, or illnesses.

TIP 31 - MAKE SURE YOU HAVE ALL THE DOCUMENTS YOU'LL NEED

It's not always rainbows and butterflies when travelling by campervan, so in the words of boy scouts everywhere, "Always be prepared". I've put together a list of essential documents you'll need to have in your van while on the road in Spain:

- Driver's licence *('carnet de conducir')*
- Van registration paperwork *('permiso de circulación')*
- ITV certificate *('ficha técnica')* - Spain's equivalent of the MOT in the UK
- Insurance Policy *('seguro')*
- European Accident Statement

TIP 32 - KNOW WHAT TO DO IF YOU BREAK DOWN OR HAVE AN ACCIDENT

If you're unlucky enough to have an accident or a breakdown on your road trip, try to stay calm and follow the usual protocol. In general, safety precautions and processes are the same for accidents and breakdowns in most European countries.

BREAKDOWNS

In the case of a breakdown, turn on your hazard lights, put on a high-vis jacket, set out warning triangles, and find a safe spot away from your vehicle to call your insurance provider. They'll send a tow truck *('grua')* to take you to the nearest garage *('taller')*. If your van needs extensive work, take all your personal objects out of the van and find nearby accommodation while you wait for it to be fixed. I recommend having your insurance policy number saved in your phone and written down somewhere safe.

ACCIDENTS

If you're involved in a traffic accident in Spain, follow the usual procedures; put on a high-vis jacket, set out warning triangles, and don't try to move injured parties. You'll then have to call 112 for emergency services (it's a toll-free number and you can speak to an operator in English) to tell them what happened and give your exact location. You will also need to fill out the European Accident Statement, and contact your insurance provider to organise a tow truck. Mechanics *('mecánicos')* are generally quite cheap in Spain, so you will most likely be back on the road in no time.

TIP 33 - TOWED OR ROBBED? MAKE SURE YOU KNOW WHICH ONE

Spain is a safe country to travel around in a campervan, but vehicle thefts and break-ins are pretty common around bigger cities. I've met quite a few van lifers who have had their van broken into or stolen around Barcelona. While this could happen anywhere in the world, it's good to be aware of places where vehicle break-ins are more common. Take extra security precautions such as leaving your van in a secured car park and double-checking your van is locked and all your access points are secure.

If you come back to your parking space and your campervan isn't there, the first step is to make sure it hasn't been towed. Look out for a triangular or rectangular yellow sticker (which will include a contact number) on the pavement where you parked. These stickers indicate that your car has been towed. If your car has been taken to the car impound *('depósito')*, you'll need to call to pay the fine before you can collect your vehicle.

If you don't see a yellow sticker or a nearby sign indicating you parked in a tow area, your van may have been stolen. In this case, or if your van has been broken into, you'll need to head to the nearest police station *('comisaría')* immediately and file a report *('hacer una denuncia')*. If your van has a GPS tracker, call the e-call service company so that they can search for your vehicle. Finally, you'll have to get in touch with your insurance company to report the theft.

Van Drama Alert

It's best to act quickly if your van gets towed! Most of the impound facilities in Spain will charge you for every hour your vehicle is impounded and sanction fines if you don't claim your vehicle within a certain time frame. It could work out to be a pretty expensive parking space. If you want to avoid this particular van drama, keep your eyes peeled for restriction signs that say *'grua'* or show a tow truck.

TIP 34 - STOCK UP ON MEDICAL SUPPLIES BEFORE YOU SET OFF

Your health is your wealth, so make sure you stock up on any prescription medication before your trip. The most common health issues van lifers face in Spain are usually from too much sun exposure, reactions to insect bites or jellyfish stings, or an upset stomach. I keep a first aid kit in the van with the essential items like plasters *('tiritas')*, antiseptic wipes *('toallitas antisépticas')*, and medication for an upset stomach in case of emergencies. If you get caught short, find the closest chemist *('farmacia')*.

If you start to feel really under the weather during your road trip, take a trip to the nearest health centre *('centro de salud')* or A&E *('urgencias')*. The healthcare system in Spain is exceptionally good and there are usually English-speaking medical staff available. You should have no problem receiving medical treatment in Spain if you have an EU medical card or a health insurance policy. Fingers crossed you won't ever have to use any of the information in this section. If you do get unlucky, then as they say in Spanish, *'¡Que te mejores!'* (get well soon).

Van Drama Alert

Having an upset stomach in the van is less than ideal, especially if you're travelling in a couple. One way to avoid tummy troubles is to be careful with your drinking water. The water supplies in most coastal areas in Spain aren't great, so you may want to stick to bottled water. We carry water purifying tablets with us to clean our water if we're drinking from mountain streams or if the water tap doesn't look clean. They're worth investing in.

Tip 35 - Learn The Lingo

I hope your road trip goes without a hitch, but just in case you run into any issues on the road I've put together some key phrases to help you out:

English	Spanish
Excuse me, is there a hospital around here?	*Perdone, ¿hay un hospital por aquí cerca?*
I have a flat tyre.	*Tengo un pinchazo.*
Do you have jump leads?	*¿Tienes pinzas?*
I'd like to report a theft.	*Quiero denunciar un robo.*
Call the police!	*¡Llama a la policía!*

SECTION 8: MEETING PEOPLE DURING YOUR VAN TRAVELS

I'm what might be known as an extroverted introvert. I enjoy socialising and meeting new people, but my social battery drains very quickly and I need a few days (or weeks!) to recover after a particularly social stint. That's probably why I love van life so much, I get plenty of alone time to recharge, but there are also plenty of opportunities to socialise. Fast-draining social battery aside, one of my favourite parts of travelling is getting to meet new people who you wouldn't normally cross paths with. I've met some incredibly interesting humans since embarking on our journey and learnt something valuable from each one. There's a big van life community in Spain and while some people enjoy the solitude, most are eager to chat with other van lifers to swap recommendations and stories from their travels.

We spend a lot of our time wild camping away from civilization and may not run into other people for days at a time. While we like our own company, after a week or two of not socialising we make an effort to get out and make new friends wherever we are. Whether you're a solo traveller or travelling in a couple, I 100%

recommend integrating into the local van life community, even if it's just a quick chat with your van neighbour in the morning. It will make your van life adventure much richer.

In the next few pages, I'll share some tips on how to meet people during your Spanish van life adventure, including a few helpful websites. While technology is a great social tool, sometimes the old-school approach is the best; smile, say hello, and make small talk about the weather. Works like a charm. As they say in Spanish, *'¡Vamos a tomar algo!'* (Let's go for a drink!).

TIP 36 - JOIN A LANGUAGE EXCHANGE NIGHT & CHAT WITH THE LOCALS

A really fun way to meet new people—especially locals—is to attend a language exchange night *('tándem'/'intercambio')*. Don't worry if you don't speak any Spanish, from my experience, most of the Spaniards who attend are happy to just practise their English. I've attended tandem nights in Seville, Madrid, Valencia, and Barcelona. They are such an enjoyable way to learn about the Spanish culture first-hand and get local knowledge of cool day trips around the area.

I haven't met many other van lifers at language exchanges, but I have met some great friends to have a coffee with next time I'm in town. If you want to join a language exchange night, check online or look out for posters in local bars, bookshops, and cafés (the local Irish bar is usually a good place to start).

Tip 37 - Join The Van Life Community On Social Media

I have a love-hate relationship with social media, but one of the biggest reasons I still use it is because it's a great tool for integrating into communities. If you use social media, you can join tons of groups to connect with fellow travellers, digital nomads, and other people with similar interests and passions. It's also a great way to find out about local events, workshops, and food festivals in the area. You'll find groups for solo female van lifers, van lifers in different regions of Spain, van lifers over thirty, and expat events across Spain. I love discovering new Spanish food festivals, gigs, open-air cinemas, and local fairs when on the road, so I regularly check out social media groups and local *'What's on'* pages to find ones that take my fancy. I mean, how else would you find an erotic tapas festival in Fuengirola, a mushroom picking festival in Extremadura, or a tomato fight in Buñol?

TIP 38 - MAKE NEW FRIENDS IN HOSTELS

From my personal experience, one of the best ways to meet fellow travellers is at hostels. Hostels can be a great alternative to motorhome areas and campsites if you're looking for a livelier atmosphere. We've stayed in a few hostel car parks and paid a reduced price to park up and use the facilities. It's always been a fun (albeit slightly noisy) experience. Alternatively, some hostels will allow you to sleep in your campervan in the car park and use the facilities in exchange for a few hours of work such as cleaning or housekeeping. If you don't fancy parking up in a hostel car park but still want to join the fun, most bigger hostels host theme nights so you can go for a drink and meet other travellers.

TIP 39 - PARTICIPATE IN WORK EXCHANGE PROGRAMMES

A big motivation for packing up city life and moving into the van was to explore a different way of life. I wanted to do more than just take a trip; I wanted to meet new people, be more creative, and learn new skills. I was especially interested in learning more about sustainable living by participating in eco-projects. This led me to research work exchange programmes. I used a website called Workaway, but I'm sure there are other similar programmes out there. This is how it works.

It connects travellers who want to exchange 4 - 5 hours of daily work for food and accommodation with hosts in the area who are looking for workers. It's a nice way to give back to the community while learning about the culture. To join, you need to pay a signup fee (we paid €49 for a joint account) and create a profile outlining the types of projects you're interested in participating in and what skills or experience you have. Once you're a member, you can contact hosts and start planning your first stay.

We participated in our first project in Portugal, working on eco-projects at a non-profit events space in the Castelo Branco valley. We met some lifelong friends and saw some incredible sustainable living projects in the local community that gave us food for thought. There's a wide variety of hosts in Spain too, so we plan to do our next exchange on the Canary Islands very soon.

Tip 40 - Learn The Lingo

Chat with the locals on your lunch breaks with these useful expressions for digital nomads.

English	Spanish
I can do odd jobs.	*Puedo hacer trabajillos.*
Can you sleep in the car park?	*¿Se puede dormir en el parking?*
What do you do?	*¿A qué te dedicas?*
Where are you from?	*¿De dónde eres?*
Nice to meet you.	*Encantada/o.*

Section 9: My Top Ten Van Life Spots In Spain

I saved the best for last. For the final ten tips in this book, I've put together a hotlist of unmissable places in Spain to visit in your campervan. Spain is a van lifer's dream, so this list could be much longer, but the title of the book is 50 Things to Know About Travelling Around Spain in a Campervan —not 500— so I've had to exercise some self-control and narrow it down. I may

105

have to turn this book into a trilogy to include all the magical van life destinations I've found in this amazing country.

For now, and in no particular order, here are my favourite van life destinations on mainland Spain. I hope you love them as much as I do.

Tip 41 - Roam The Land Of Quixote In Las Lagunas De R_.._ Ciudad Real

Possibly one of Spain's best-kept secrets, this incredible national park boasts fifteen lagoons, waterfalls, and wildlife galore.

WHERE IS IT?

Just a three-hour drive from Madrid, located between Albacete and Ciudad Real.

WHY I LOVE IT

Driving through the national park is surreal, it's like you've left Spain and have been transported to South America. Aside from the stunning landscape and diverse wildlife, this land is steeped in culture. Spanish Author, Miguel de Cervantes, set two chapters of his epic tale, *Don Quixote,* here. Widely considered one of the best novels ever written, roaming Quixote land is a must for any literature buff.

BE SURE TO CHECK OUT

The park is home to the well-known Montesinos Caves, where the novel's much-loved hero, Don Quixote, spent a night. The caves are open to visitors and worth a visit during your stay.

COORDINATES OF WHERE WE STAYED:
39.062771, -3.007870

We spent three days in this little slice of heaven. As it's a national park, sleeping in your campervan inside the park is forbidden, but there's a motorhome area just a short drive away where you can stay overnight for free.

Tip 42 - Get Lost In Cabo de Gata National Park, Almería

Cabo de Gata is one of the most beautiful national parks in Spain and home to some of the best beaches in the country. Thanks to its unique landscape, it's a popular shooting spot for spaghetti Westerns.

WHERE IS IT?

It's located on Spain's southeast coast, the only area in Europe to have a hot desert climate.

WHY I LOVE IT

The amazing beaches, quaint fishing towns, breathtaking landscape, salt flats with flamingos, and a huge variety of wildlife. You could spend months exploring this idyllic corner of Spain.

BE SURE TO CHECK OUT

The beaches. There are so many stunning beaches and coves in the national park. My favourites were Playa de los Genoveses, Playa de los Muertos, and Arrecife de la Sirena (look out for the old railway that goes straight into the sea).

COORDINATES OF WHERE WE STAYED
37.0058682, -1.8893651
Wild camping in Cabo de Gata national park is prohibited, so we spent our days exploring all it has to offer and then drove to nearby Carboneras (on the border of the park) to sleep for free by the beach.

TIP 43 - STROLL AROUND THE PICTURESQUE TOWN OF PALS, GIRONA

There were heaps of fantastic van life destinations on the Costa Brava, but there's just something special about the picturesque medieval town of Pals. Pals is listed as a Historic Artistic Site of Spain.

WHERE IS IT?
Pals is perched six kilometres inland from the Costa Brava coastline in the province of Girona.

WHY I LOVE IT
The beautiful gothic old quarter, the relaxed atmosphere, and the views of the coastline.

BE SURE TO CHECK OUT

Lose yourself in the historic old quarter, visit the nearby beaches, or take a look around the numerous artisanal shops. If you have time, take a drive to the neighbouring town of Peratallada, just over eight kilometres away. It's another beautiful medieval town and a perfect place to stop off for a spot of lunch. From Pals, we drove to the pretty coastal town of Tamariu and spent a few days hiking along the breathtaking Cami de Ronda coastal path. Simply incredible.

COORDINATES OF WHERE WE STAYED

41.9711990, 3.1467000

We found a free car park just outside the old town in Pals. Even though it was next to a restaurant, it was very quiet and we had no issues staying for a few nights.

Tip 44 - Watch The Sunset In Romantic Ronda, Málaga

With panoramic views, a charming town, and a bridge set over the impressive El Tajo gorge, it's no wonder that Ernest Hemingway fell in love with Ronda. Known for being one of the most romantic towns in Spain, Ronda is sure to steal your heart.

WHERE IS IT?

Ronda is just over an hour's drive inland from Marbella. It's in the mountains, so be prepared for some stunning scenery and winding mountain roads.

WHY I LOVE IT

The incredible views, the relaxed vibe, and the delicious food. There's magic in the air in Ronda. I'm not the only one who loves it, Ronda is the third most visited town in Andalucía.

BE SURE TO CHECK OUT

There are so many things to see and do in Ronda; trek down into the El Tajo gorge, watch a sunset from the Puente Nuevo bridge, check out the Arab baths, and visit one of the oldest bullrings in Spain. If you fancy a day trip, deep in the mountains just a thirty-minute drive from Ronda is the village of Júzcar, also known as the Smurf Village. Originally one of the white villages of Andalucía, in 2011 all of the buildings in the village were painted blue to celebrate the premiere of the Smurfs (*'los Pitufos'*) movie. We stopped off for lunch and spent a surreal afternoon strolling around the smurf-themed village. A unique experience.

COORDINATES OF WHERE WE STAYED
36.7220100, -5.1720970
We couldn't find many free camping spots in Ronda, so we decided to stay in this motorhome area which was a twenty-five-minute walk to the town. It's a great motorhome area and reasonably priced, but a bit far from the town and the roads weren't well lit up at night.

TIP 45 - VISIT ALTEA, ALICANTE, THE SANTORINI OF SPAIN

Altea's whitewashed houses, charming old town, serene beaches, and rich artistic culture make it one of the prettiest cities on the Costa Blanca. I try to come to Altea at least once a year to unwind, although we usually stay just outside of Altea city near L'Olla beach.

113

WHERE IS IT?

Altea is located on the Costa Blanca, less than an hour north of Alicante. You'll find this pearl nestled between the popular seaside resorts of Benidorm and Calpe.

WHY I LOVE IT

With its white buildings covered in brightly coloured flowers, blue-domed roofs, and stunning sea views, Altea has earned its reputation as the Santorini of Spain. I love visiting Altea in October and spending a few days relaxing on the beach.

BE SURE TO CHECK OUT

Soak up the sun on the beach, rent a stand-up paddleboard, read a book on a sunny terrace, visit a museum, or explore the heaving art scene. You won't get bored in Altea. Altea is just a short drive from a couple of other beautiful coastal cities on the Costa Blanca. Take a day trip to see the colourful buildings in the beach town of Villajoyosa or spend a few days in nearby Calpe, climbing the towering Penyal d'Ifach rock and flamingo watching.

COORDINATES OF WHERE WE STAYED

38.6204847, -0.0243588

This free car park is outside of Altea town overlooking L'Olla beach and L'Olla island. It's a five-minute walk from the rocky dog beach (Bella's favourite place). There's a beach bar right below the car park and you'll find more bars and restaurants as you walk along the beachfront.

TIP 46 - ENJOY SECLUDED BEACHES IN IDYLLIC ISLA CRISTINA, HUELVA

If you're a beach lover, but you like to avoid crowds, then Isla Cristina is right up your alley. This small coastal town is the perfect place to relax on the beach with a good book, eat fresh seafood, and take a break from the bustling beaches in Andalucía. An introvert's paradise.

WHERE IS IT?

Isla Cristina is right on the border with Portugal. It's a twenty-minute drive from the border town of Ayamonte in South West Andalucía.

WHY I LOVE IT

I love a wild beach and Isla Cristina didn't disappoint. We visited in July and were delighted to find Isla

Cristina was much less touristy than most other beaches in Andalucía, even during the high season.

BE SURE TO CHECK OUT
Explore the unspoilt beaches of Isla Cristina and eat some fried fish on the seafront before watching the sunset over the Atlantic. If you fancy a break from lounging on beautiful beaches, take a trip to the salt flats to see the amazing array of flora and fauna, or check out the Carnival Museum.

COORDINATES OF WHERE WE STAYED
37.2007512, -7.2905640
We stayed in a free car park right next to the beach for five days without any issues. There were public showers, beach bars, restaurants, and shops all within a fifteen-minute walk from where we parked up.

TIP 47 - TOUR THE MOST ICONIC *'PUEBLOS BLANCOS'* IN ANDALUCÍA

No Spanish road trip would be complete without touring at least a few of the iconic white villages *('pueblos blancos')* in Andalucía. Andalucía is famous for its quaint villages of whitewashed buildings decorated with brightly coloured flowers and mazes of narrow cobbled streets. There are too many *'pueblos blancos'* to name them all, but I've chosen a few of my favourites.

WHERE IS IT?

The famous whitewashed villages, or *'pueblos blancos',* span southern Andalucía from Málaga to Cádiz. There is a popular driving route that takes you through the most notable ones over a few days.

WHY I LOVE IT

There's just something quintessentially Spanish about the emblematic white villages with their bright colours, laid back atmosphere, and maze-like streets.

Setenil de las Bodegas in Cádiz is one of the most famous *'pueblos blancos'* on the route. Setenil de las Bodegas is a small town, well-known for the whitewashed houses built into and underneath remarkable rock overhangs. If you visit in winter, you can even see stalactites hanging from the rocks. It's a sight to behold and definitely worth stopping off for lunch and strolling down *Calle Cuevas de la Sombra* and *Calle Cuevas del Sol* for an up-close look at the rock overhang.

Nerja and Frigiliana are two of the best known *'pueblos blancos'* in the province of Málaga and are well worth visiting. The outstanding views from the *'Balcón de Europa'* in Nerja are reason alone to pay a visit. Take a trip to the famous Nerja caves, followed by a lazy lunch looking over the Mediterranean, and round the day off with a refreshing dip.

Make sure you hop on the tourist train in Frigiliana for a fun tour of this gorgeous mountain village and do a spot of shopping in the many local boutiques.

From Frigiliana, take a short drive through the mountains to the lost village of Acebuchal. The inhabitants of this rural hamlet were forced to flee by the Guardia Civil in 1948, leaving it abandoned for fifty years. In 1998, the son of one of the original inhabitants returned and began breathing life back into the lost village. Now it's a fully-restored, pretty little hamlet hidden away in the mountains. There's one tavern in the village that serves heavenly food. Go check it out. It really is like stepping back in time. I'm talking donkeys and mules on the streets, no television (satellite only), and no phone signal, so bring cash as you can't pay by card.

COORDINATES OF WHERE WE STAYED
36.8021236, -3.9123971
We found a free camping spot in the mountains overlooking Frigiliana where we spent a few peaceful nights.

TIP 48 - RECHARGE YOUR BATTERIES IN THE PYRENEES

We spent ten days exploring the stunning Spanish side of the Pyrenees, starting in Zugarramurdi and making our way east. I could easily have spent months touring the Pyrenees and can't wait to go back.

WHERE IS IT?

The peaks of the Pyrenees mark the border between Spain and France.

WHY I LOVE IT

Rugged countryside, pretty ski towns, delicious food and wine, incredible views, wildlife, and a plethora of hiking trails. There is something for everyone in the Pyrenees.

BE SURE TO CHECK OUT

The Pyrenees is home to an abundance of hiking trails and beautiful ski towns, such as Panticosa and neighbouring Sallent de Gállego, to stop off for a well-deserved drink after a hard day's hiking. If you fancy something a bit different, just five minutes from the French border is the town of Zugarramurdi. Zugarramurdi made its way into the history books for being named as a site of occult activity in the Basque witch trials in Logroño in the 17th century. The town has embraced its witchy past and opened a fascinating Witch Museum and self-guided tours of the Witch Caves.

COORDINATES OF WHERE WE STAYED

43.270633, -1.541328

In Zugarramurdi, we stayed in a large hotel car park just a two-minute walk from the town square. There are several free motorhome areas in the Pyrenees, so you can normally rock up and find somewhere to sleep.

TIP 49 - EXPLORE ROMAN RUINS BY THE BEACH IN BOLONIA, CÁDIZ

Not every day do you find a beach with sparkling turquoise water, white sands, mighty sand dunes, and Roman ruins lining the beach. That, along with the captivating views of Africa (it looks close enough to touch), make Bolonia beach truly unique.

WHERE IS IT?

Bolonia beach *('Playa de Bolonia')* is tucked away in Spain's southernmost tip.

WHY I LOVE IT

Its wild beauty, super friendly locals, and astounding Roman ruins. We spent a few relaxing days there and I can't wait to go back. A word of warning, those dunes are tough to walk up in the midday heat.

BE SURE TO CHECK OUT
Feel like a big kid again and scale *'La Gran Duna'* (the great sand dune) on the western side of the beach for magnificent views of Africa, go snorkelling in the crystal clear waters, walk around the Roman ruins of Baelo Claudia, catch some rays on the beach, or chill out in the shade at one of the surrounding beach bars. There's plenty to keep you busy on Bolonia beach.

COORDINATES OF WHERE WE STAYED
36.087131, -5.769637
We spent a few nights sleeping in a free car park right next to the beach.

TIP 50 - VISIT THE GHOST TOWN OF LA MUSSARA, COSTA BRAVA

If abandoned villages with eerie pasts and spectacular views are your thing, then add La Mussara to your itinerary. Since being abandoned under strange circumstances in 1959, the village has become overgrown with brambles and is now in ruins. Known as the ghost town where people go missing, legend has it La Mussara is home to otherworldly activity. Lovers of the supernatural frequent La Mussara every Halloween in the search for things that go bump in the night.

WHERE IS IT?

From Tarragona, La Mussara is a fifty-minute drive into the Serra de la Mussara mountain range.

WHY I LOVE IT

As if reports of missing people, phantom horse sounds in the middle of the night, a mysterious fog that sweeps over the village without warning, and rumours of a rock portal to another dimension weren't enough to pique my interest, the views from La Mussara (when the fog clears) are out of this world.

123

BE SURE TO CHECK OUT

After wandering around the ruins of the old village and being wowed by the views, check out the countless hiking trails around La Mussara or try your hand at rock climbing. Just be careful with the fog! If you're feeling adventurous, you could even hunt for the rock that is supposed to transport you to another dimension.

COORDINATES OF WHERE WE STAYED

41.2537906, 1.0311706

In the abandoned town, right next to the ruins, there's a small mountain refuge called *'Refugi La Mussara'* which has a bar, restaurant, Wi-Fi, bathrooms, and bedrooms. We stayed in the garden and paid €6 each for the night.

SECTION 10: A DAY IN THE LIFE OF A VAN LIFER IN SPAIN

If you're toying with the idea of living in your van on a more long-term basis but you're not sure if it's for you, I've put together an outline of a typical day. I hope it helps you to visualise what full-time van life might look like.

With this book, I really want to give an accurate, warts and all idea of what long-term van life is like. So even though a typical day in my life is the way I've described it below, not every day is like that. Van living comes with its own maintenance. Every four or five days, we have a van maintenance morning where we go and fill our water tanks, empty our grey and black water, buy groceries, and do laundry. We try to split the tasks to speed the process up, but it can still take a full morning.

08:30 - WAKE UP

I'm not an early riser, so I usually wake up around 08:30 unless it's very hot or we're parked in a noisy area. We take our bench down immediately (we use it to extend our bed), and put it back under the bed so we have floor space.

08:45 - FEED AND WALK BELLA

I feed Bella and take her on a short walk to do her business.

09:00 - HAVE BREAKFAST

I usually make breakfast in the van. I like to go for something quick and easy like cereal or yoghurt with berries and a cup of tea. After breakfast, we clear up our dishes.

09:30 - TIDY THE VAN

Our van is small, so it can get messy pretty quickly. After breakfast, we'll usually make the bed, sweep the floor, and put away any clothes that are lying about. We also try to charge electronics during the day when we have the most solar power.

10:00 - GO EXPLORING

Once the van is spick and span, we usually explore the area. We'll either take Bella for a long walk along the beach, go for a hike, or stroll into the nearest town. If we're moving on, we'll pack up the van and hit the road. We try to limit our drives to under three hours per day, so we get to spend more time outside and Bella isn't cooped up in the van all day.

13:00 - GET LUNCH READY

If we're in a town or on the beachfront, we'll often go
out for lunch to soak in our surroundings, grab some
Wi-Fi, and use the bathrooms. When we're staying in
the mountains or further off the grid, we'll make lunch
in the van.

14:00 - WORK

I much prefer to work in the afternoons and use my
mornings to get out and about. My typical work
schedule is from 2 pm to 7 pm. I normally work from
the van, tethering the internet from my mobile phone. If
we're at a campsite or in a busier town, I'll occasionally
look for a quiet place to work, but I find it pretty
comfortable to work in the van as long as I take regular
breaks to stretch and walk around.

17:00 - FEED BELLA AND GO FOR A QUICK STROLL

I take a break from work around 5 pm to feed and walk
Bella. If I'm not too busy with work, I might stop for
the day and read a book or relax.

19:00 - DINNER TIME

We eat dinner in the van most evenings. After I finish
work, around 7 pm, we'll start making dinner before it

gets dark. In the summer months when it stays brighter for longer, we tend to eat a little later. Cooking dinner, eating, and doing the washing up usually takes around an hour or an hour and a half.

20:00 - RELAX
After dinner, we usually relax in the van and watch a series. If we're near the beach, we like to take a blanket down and watch the sunset. In colder months, we sometimes turn on our little heater and snuggle up with a good movie.

22:00 - TAKE BELLA FOR A WALK
We take Bella for a quick walk around 10 pm so she can do her business and have one final run around before bed.

23:00 - PUT UP THE BENCH AND LIGHTS OUT
At around 11 pm, we get our bench out from under the bed and put it up for sleeping. The bench goes at the foot of the bed to give us extra legroom and has to be done last because once it's up we can't get into our cupboards. It's not ideal, but it has become part of our nightly routine and we barely notice anymore.

SECTION 11: MY VAN ESSENTIALS

Choosing what to pack for your trip can be a nightmare, especially if, like me, minimalism doesn't come naturally to you. Over the years, I have honed my packing skills and while I still tend to overpack, I am definitely now a reformed hoarder. The biggest advice I can give you when it comes to packing is to think about the type of trip you're taking. If you're going to spend your time camping by beaches and seaside towns, then you will need very different gear than if you're going to spend a month wild camping in the mountains.

To give you a starting point, I've made a list of some of my essentials that have greatly enhanced my time on the road:

- EU Plug Adapter
- CEE Adapter (most campsites that we've stayed in require this type of adapter to plug into the electricity box)
- Solar shower
- Eco-friendly toiletries (if you plan to use your solar shower in nature)
- Gas stove and spare gas canisters
- A saucepan and frying pan
- Cutlery (we have two each of everything)

- Magnetic hooks (No idea how we ever lived without these!)
- A retractable colander (this fits across our sink and doubles up as a drying rack for dishes)
- Power banks
- Water purifying tablets (if you plan to do wild camping or long hikes)
- A fridge or coolbox (especially if you're travelling around Spain during summer)
- A waterproof jacket and a hoodie
- Booties for swimming (great for rocky beaches and rivers)
- Insulated window covers (probably one of the best investments we've made)
- Travel insurance
- Foldable chairs
- A mosquito net
- Mosquito repellent
- Environmentally-friendly suncream
- A sun hat
- A beach umbrella (if travelling during the summer months)
- A headlamp

SECTION 13: IF I COULD TURN BACK TIME - THINGS I'D LIKE TO CHANGE IN OUR VAN

You know what they say, hindsight is 20/20. We're delighted with the van overall, but having spent three years living in it, there are a couple of design flaws that we'd love to change or do differently next time around. If you're in the process of planning your campervan conversion, I hope this section offers some inspiration, or at the very least, steers you away from a few common blunders.

Basically, this section contains five tips I would give myself if I could go back in time.

GET BIGGER WATER TANKS

We currently have 50L of fresh water and a 50L tank for grey water, however, we go through it really quickly. Due to space restrictions, we went for smaller tanks, but ideally, I would love to have a 100L freshwater tank. Our water tanks aren't in the most accessible place (more on that later), so it would be fantastic to be able to fill our tank with more water, less often. We fill an extra 25L jerry can with water for our solar shower so we always have enough, but a larger, fixed freshwater tank is a must-have in our next campervan.

INVEST IN A PORTABLE SOLAR PANEL

The shape of our roof and the size of the van meant that we only had room for one solar panel and one roof vent. The solar panel generally produces enough electricity to charge everything we have, including my laptop. However, after a week of rain in Portugal, I decided to add a portable solar panel to my van wishlist. We'll be able to hang it outside the van or put it on the dashboard for extra power, folding it down when not in use.

GO FOR A FIXED BED WITH SLATS FOR COMFORT & AIR CIRCULATION

As I mentioned earlier in the book, we opted for a bed that doubles as a table and benches which we never use. One of the biggest lessons I've learned is that since air can't circulate well, beds without slats tend to have a buildup of condensation. During the colder months, we've noticed that the bottom of our foam mattress is damp in the mornings and we have to dry it out in the sun. It's not the end of the world though, after chatting to some other van lifers, we've discovered a few hacks to solve the issue. Leaving the windows open a crack helps to reduce the condensation and putting an anti-condensation mat under the foam mattress lets the air circulate. Next time, I want a higher, fixed bed with a full-size mattress and more space under the bed for storage.

MAKE OUR BENCHES MORE ACCESSIBLE

Perhaps the biggest design flaw we've realised with our van is how the benches that hold the water tanks are designed. To fill up our water tanks, we need to lift up our foam mattress and the lid of our bench. This makes filling our tanks much more of an effort than it needs to be. Our plan is to cut a hole in the side of the bench so we can pop the hose in and easily fill the tanks without having to lift the mattress. I've seen quite a few vans that have a switch inside to empty their grey water tanks. This is another little luxury that I would love to incorporate into our next van conversion.

INVEST IN A COMPOSTING TOILET

I'm like *'Goldilocks And The Three Bears'* when it comes to choosing the right toilet for our van. We started off without a toilet in the van, relying on public bathrooms or the great outdoors. This wasn't ideal (sometimes nature calls at the most inopportune moments), so we bought a portapotty. The portapotty works well, but it needs to be emptied every few days. As it contains chemicals, we need to find a designated area to empty it which doesn't really suit our lifestyle in the van. I was originally put off by the price, but one of the next investments I want to make for the van is a composting toilet. After chatting with other van lifers, it seems like the best throne for our castle on wheels.

SECTION 14: OUR TOP VAN LIFE RECIPES

Spanish food is delicious and very well-priced, but when we're camping away from cities and the coastline we mostly cook in our van. Preparing our food in the van is cheaper and gives us the freedom to go further off the grid. We tend to steer away from cooking raw meat unless we know we have access to hot water, and instead opt for cured meats, vegetables, and legumes. Spain has an amazing assortment of seasonal fruit and vegetables, so be sure to buy from local greengrocers whenever you can and not just the large chain supermarkets.

Here are a few of my favourite, failsafe recipes to inspire you.

PESTO PASTA WITH JAMÓN SERRANO, MOZZARELLA, AND TOMATOES

Simple to prepare and delicious, this is one of our go-to van meals. Cooking in your van means limited counter and sink space, so one-pot meals like this are perfect. Although some people don't like to eat pasta in the heat, I personally always have room for pasta.

This recipe is for homemade green pesto (no food processor needed), but you could easily substitute it for a jar of ready-made pesto, available in all the big supermarkets.

Ingredients:

- Mozzarella cheese - We go for the small mozzarella balls so we don't have to cut and use more cutlery
- Serrano ham - Available in any supermarket or butcher's in Spain
- Fresh cherry tomatoes
- 2 cloves of garlic, finely sliced
- A handful of spinach, washed
- Dried pasta, we usually use farfalle

Pesto ingredients:

- ¼ cup finely chopped Pine nuts
- 4 cups fresh basil leaves
- 1 garlic clove, minced
- ½ cup extra virgin olive oil
- ¼ cup grated parmesan cheese

Green pesto

Method:

1. Remove the stems from the basil leaves
2. Chop the basil finely, while incorporating the minced garlic
3. Combine the basil, garlic, pinenuts, olive oil, and parmesan cheese into a ziplock bag, squeeze all the air out and seal it shut
4. Roll a mug or mason jar over the sandwich bag of pesto to crush the ingredients more
5. Transfer to a bowl and pop in the fridge to let the flavours meld
6. Once the flavours have melded together, season to taste

Method:

1. Cook your pasta al dente, following the instructions on the packet
2. Finely slice the serrano ham and set it aside
3. Heat some olive oil on medium-high heat and add the sliced garlic to cook for 2 minutes
4. Add the cherry tomatoes, stirring occasionally for 6 - 8 minutes or until the tomatoes burst and release their juices
5. Stir in the spinach and cook until wilted
6. Add the mozzarella cheese, stirring through until the mozzarella starts to melt
7. Stir in the cooked pasta and the pesto, mixing everything
8. Add the serrano ham, making sure it's evenly distributed
9. Serve hot with some fresh bread

ENSALADA MIXTA

'Ensalada mixta' (mixed salad) is a staple dish in
Spain. When eating out, Spaniards will usually order a
big mixed salad for the table. The ingredients of an
'Ensalada mixta' vary slightly depending on the region,
but this recipe is the most classic version. The secrets to
a great *'Ensalada mixta'* are good quality products and
just the right amount of dressing.

Ingredients:
- ½ head of Lettuce (iceberg or romaine)
- 2 large tomatoes
- 1 carrot
- 2 - 3 hard-boiled eggs
- 1 small can of sweetcorn
- ½ jar of white asparagus
- 1 small can of green olives
- 1 can of tuna or anchovies
- ½ onion
- Red wine vinegar
- Extra virgin olive oil
- Salt

Method:

1. Boil the eggs for around 8 - 10 minutes until hard-boiled, leave to cool
2. Wash and dry the fruit and vegetables
3. Slice the onions
4. Cut the tomatoes into wedges
5. Roughly tear up the lettuce
6. Drain the olives, asparagus, sweetcorn, and tuna
7. Finely grate the carrot
8. Place all the ingredients on a large plate or in a bowl
9. Peel the shell off the eggs, slice into wedges and place on top of the salad ingredients
10. Drizzle with olive oil, red wine vinegar, and salt
11. Dig in and enjoy

SPANISH TOMATO TOAST WITH SERRANO HAM

'Tostada con tomate y jamón serrano' is the most iconic Spanish breakfast there is. You can find it all over Spain, and I recommend going to a café and ordering it with a *'café con leche'* at least once on your trip. Even though it's cheap enough to eat out every morning (we're talking a couple of euros), I love making this breakfast in the van. It's quick to make and there's little cleanup required which is perfect when cooking in a small space with a limited water supply.

Essentially, it's a piece of toasted bread drizzled with olive oil and topped with fresh tomato spread. In many parts of Spain, especially in Andalucía, you can order it with a slice of Serrano ham on top. As with most Spanish cuisine, the key is to use high-quality ingredients and keep the rest simple.

If you want to make your own Spanish-style tomato toast, here's how.

Ingredients:

- 6 - 8 slices of crusty bread (use a baguette, not sliced pan)
- 3 - 4 medium to large tomatoes
- 1 clove of garlic
- 4 teaspoons of extra virgin olive oil
- Salt
- Serrano ham (optional)

Method:

1. Wash the tomatoes and pat dry
2. Cut the tomatoes in half and grate them finely
3. Toast the bread (I use a RidgeMonkey which is perfect for toasting bread on the gas stove)
4. Peel the garlic and slice in half
5. Rub the garlic on the toasted slices of bread
6. Spread the grated tomato mixture evenly on each slice
7. Sprinkle a pinch of salt
8. Drizzle around half a teaspoon of olive oil
9. Top with slices of Serrano ham
10. Wash it down with some fresh orange juice or a coffee

A SPANISH TASTING PLATTER

Ingredients:

- An assortment of cheeses (I recommend some tasty Manchego cheese)
- Olives
- Grapes
- An assortment of meats (Spain is famous for its cured meats like *jamón Serrano* and *chorizo)*
- Breadsticks
- Gazpacho (This refreshing cold soup is always best homemade, but tricky to make in a campervan. There are plenty of delicious options in the local supermarkets and it's perfect for hot summer days)
- Anchovies *'Boquerones en vinagre'* (Delicious when served on top of a sliced baguette, *'una barra',* with some fresh tomato slices)
- We usually add any other seasonal fruit, like pomegranates or melon

Method:

1. Pop all your ingredients on a wooden chopping board
2. Serve with some fresh crusty bread drizzled with extra virgin olive oil
3. Get stuck in

SECTION 15: OTHER HELPFUL RESOURCES

I don't know about you, but for me, half of the fun of travelling is planning. I love researching our next spot and finding useful resources. Here are a few that have made our lives easier.

afourwheelhome.com

Check out my website to follow our travels. You'll find heaps of content on van DIY, my favourite van life destinations, my struggles to become a minimalist, and my mission to live a more sustainable lifestyle.

Duolingo app

This is a great app for brushing up on your Spanish skills before and during your trip. It's a fun way to learn the basics so you can order meals and communicate with the locals during your trip.

Furgovw.org

If you speak Spanish, this website-cum-forum is a great resource for connecting with the local van life community. As well as creating a forum for sharing tips and questions about van life in Spain, they also use the site to organise events and meetups across Spain. It's a great way to meet other like-minded travellers on the road.

Park4Night app

This app is a great way to find places to stay overnight in your van. You'll find a mix of campsites, motorhome areas, and wild camping spots. Fellow van lifers leave rankings and reviews on the spots they have visited so you can get a good idea of what to expect.

Refill app

If like me, you hate buying plastic water bottles, then this eco-friendly app is for you. It maps out shops, businesses, fountains, and transport hubs in the area where you can refill your water bottle for free. No plastic needed.

TelPark app

This app allows you to pay the parking meter from wherever you are without having to go back to your van. It's perfect for Pay & Display parking in big cities.

workaway.info

Workaway is a website for travellers who want to exchange four-five hours of daily work in exchange for food and board. The Workawayers stay with a host, usually on farms, hostels, or family homes and have the opportunity to learn about the culture, participate in language exchanges, and pick up (or share) some new skills.

SECTION 16: TRIVIA

TEST YOUR SPANISH SKILLS

You'll run into English speakers in most parts of Spain, but it's always good to make an effort to pick up a few phrases in the local language when travelling.

Test your Spanish skills with this trivia quiz to see how many of the most important van life vocabulary words and expressions you can remember. You'll find the answers below.

1) How do you say "Have a nice trip!" in Spanish?
2) What is the Spanish word for "toll"?
3) If someone says *'encantado/a'* to you, what do they mean?
4) How do you say "driving licence" in Spanish?
5) How do you say "police station" in Spanish?
6) What is *'una furgoneta'* in English?
7) What is the Spanish word for a "fine"?
8) How do you say "laundrette" in Spanish?
9) Sleeping inside your campervan, with no objects hanging outside is known as what in Spanish?
10) How do you say "A&E/Emergency department" in Spanish?

ANSWERS:

1) ¡Buen viaje!
2) Peaje
3) Nice to meet you
4) Carnet (de conducir)
5) Comisaría
6) A van or campervan
7) Una multa
8) Lavandería
9) Pernoctar
10) Urgencias

SECTION 17: GET IN THE MOOD: THE SOUNDTRACK TO OUR ROAD TRIP

No unforgettable road trip is complete without some great music. Here is a list of our Top 24 Campervan Classics that always get us in the mood for our next big adventure.

1. On the Road Again by Canned Heat
2. In the Summertime by Mungo Jerry
3. I've Got to Use My Imagination by Gladys Knight & The Pips
4. A Message to You Rudy by The Specials
5. Green Onions by Booker T & The M.G's
6. A Minha Menina by The Bees
7. Heaven's Open by Mike Oldfield
8. Road to Nowhere by Talking Heads
9. Blister in The Sun by Violent Femmes
10. Drive My Car by The Beatles
11. Life Is A Highway by Tom Cochrane
12. Take It Easy by Eagles
13. Hotel California by Gipsy Kings
14. Dreams by The Cranberries

153

15. Mr Blue Sky by Electric Light Orchestra

16. Dreams by Fleetwood Mac

17. My Sweet Lord by George Harrison

18. I Can See Clearly Now by Johnny Nash

19. Ooh La La by Faces

20. Send Me on My Way by Rusted Root

21. The Man in Me by Bob Dylon

22. Jessica by Allman Brothers Band

23. Entre Dos Aguas by Paco de Lucía

24. Tamacun by Rodrigo y Gabriela

Thanks for reading. See you down the road!

READ OTHER
50 THINGS TO KNOW
BOOKS

Stay up to date with new releases on Amazon:

https://amzn.to/2VPNGr7

CZYKPublishing.com

We'd love to hear what you think about our content!
Please leave your honest review of this book on
Amazon and Goodreads. We appreciate your positive
and constructive feedback. Thank you.

Manufactured by Amazon.com.au
Sydney, New South Wales, Australia